THE 3 MINUTE GRATITUDE JOURNAL

WITH MOTIVATIONAL QUOTES

90 Days to Cultivate
Gratitude and Mindfulness

We would love to hear from you!
Please, consider leaving a review with your opinions and recommendations.

Copyright © 2020 by Skribent

All rights reserved. No part of this book may be reproduced or used in any manner without written permission of the copyright owner except for the use of quotations in a book review.

First paperback edition October 2020

Second paperback edition January 2021

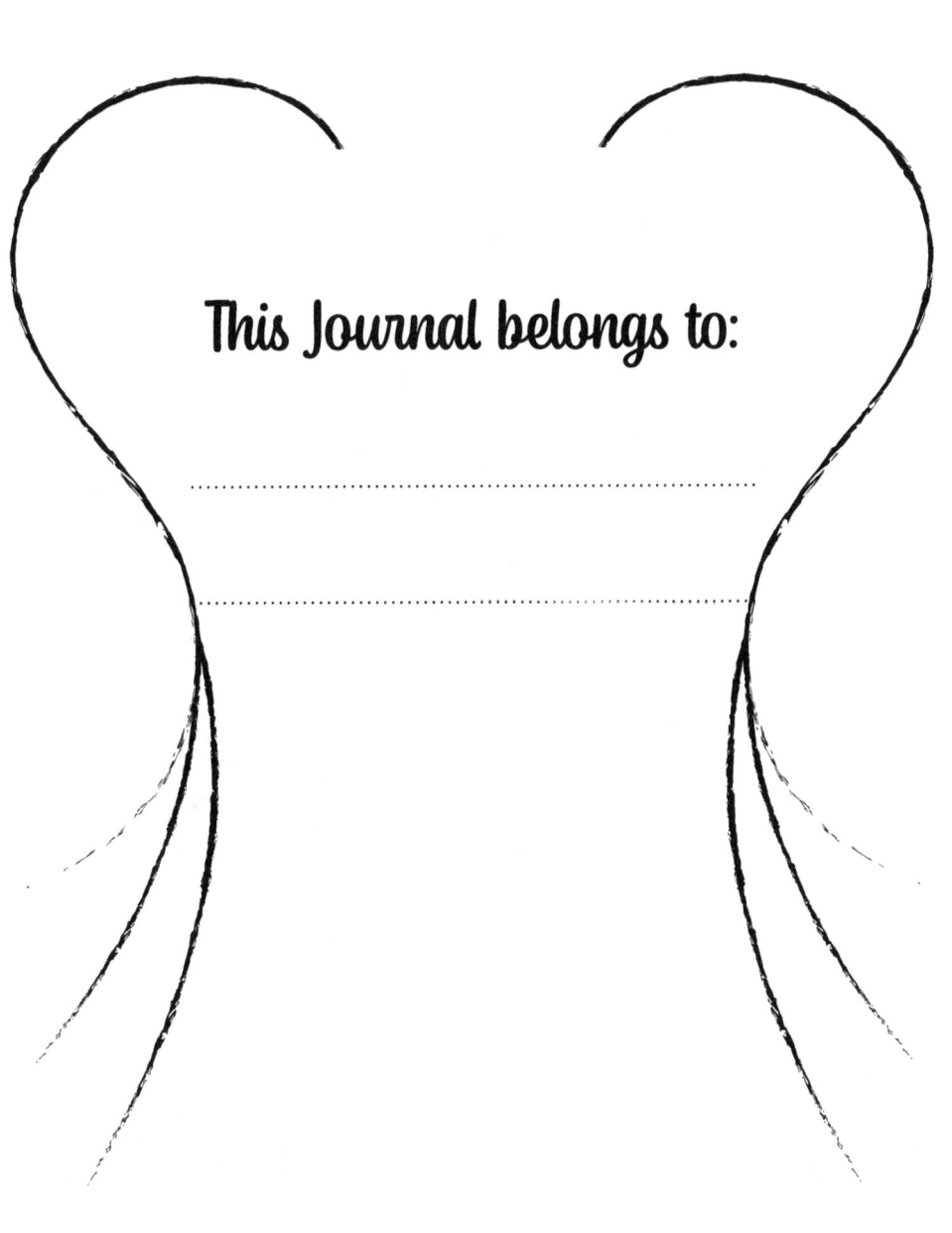

This Journal belongs to:

....

....

Gratitude....What a wonderful word!

Gratitude is the feeling of appreciation for our life, our friends and family, the small little details that surround us. Moreover, it boosts your happiness and increases your self-esteem.

Although is an amazing sensation, it is so difficult nowadays to feel grateful. Just think about this whole year... It seems almost impossible to embrace gratitude in the present moment.

However, even when times are tough, you should always adopt an attitude of gratitude and enjoy the unexpected joys and surprises of daily life.

This journal will help you feel grateful and form habits for a lifetime. It will train you to focus on all the important things. Every day you will have the opportunity to practice gratitude and learn to **identify and appreciate yourself and the world around you**.

Once in a while, we need some motivation in all our lives. That is why at the beginning of every daily page you will find **all-time inspirational quotes** from some of the most important people in the world. These phrases will encourage you and help you reach your potential.

Furthermore, we will **challenge you**. We intend to challenge you to take action, to be proactive, and be the best version of yourself.

Sometimes, however, you might feel the need to just express yourself and forget about everything else. This is **not the time to hold anything back**, so use **"Express your feelings"** pages to pour out all your emotions. Draw, doodle, write...

One last detail, every 30 days you will have the chance to think about the past days, reflect on all the beautiful moments you enjoyed and just be grateful. It's the perfect exercise to keep your perspective intact and appreciate the big and the small things that color every day of your life.

Final advice:

Set a time frame and try to form a habit. Decide the time frame that better suits you and don't forget about it.

Feel free to write anything. This is **your** journal, **you can express fully all your feelings and thoughts**.

Thanks a lot for deciding to embark on this journey. Hopefully, it will be a wonderful trip full of blessings and sweet memories.

"Social scientists have found that the fastest way to feel happiness is to practice gratitude."

Chip Conley

I am grateful for: Date   /   /

_____
_____
_____
_____

Things that made me laugh:

_____
_____
_____

Memorable moments:

_____
_____
_____

One word to describe how you're feeling:

_____

A positive thought:

_____
_____
_____

> *"Gratitude is merely the secret hope of further favors."*
>
> Francois de La Rochefoucauld

I am grateful for: Date   /   /
_____
_____
_____

Things that made me laugh:
_____
_____
_____

Memorable moments:
_____
_____
_____

One word to describe how you're feeling:
_____

A positive thought:
_____
_____
_____

> "The essence of all beautiful art, all great art, is gratitude."
>
> Friedrich Nietzsche

I am grateful for: Date   /   /

_____
_____
_____
_____

Things that made me laugh:

_____
_____
_____

Memorable moments:

_____
_____
_____

One word to describe how you're feeling:

_____

A positive thought:

_____
_____
_____

> "What a precious privilege it is to be alive - to breathe, to think, to enjoy, to love."
> Marcus Aurelius

I am grateful for: Date   /   /

_____
_____
_____
_____

Things that made me laugh:

_____
_____
_____

Memorable moments:

_____
_____
_____

One word to describe how you're feeling:

_____

A positive thought:

_____
_____
_____

"Hope has a good memory, gratitude a bad one."

Baltasar Gracian

I am grateful for: Date   /   /
___
___
___

Things that made me laugh:
___
___
___

Memorable moments:
___
___
___

One word to describe how you're feeling:
___

A positive thought:
___
___
___

> "Nature's beauty is a gift that cultivates appreciation and gratitude."
> Louis Schwartzberg

I am grateful for:　　　　　　　　Date　/　/

_____
_____
_____
_____

Things that made me laugh:

_____
_____
_____

Memorable moments:

_____
_____
_____

One word to describe how you're feeling:

_____

A positive thought:

_____
_____

Tell someone you love how much they mean to you

> *"Always give without remembering and always receive without forgetting."*
> Brian Tracy

I am grateful for: Date   /   /

_____
_____
_____

Things that made me laugh:

_____
_____
_____

Memorable moments:

_____
_____
_____

One word to describe how you're feeling:

_____

A positive thought:

_____
_____
_____

> *"To live a life fulfilled, reflect on the things you have with gratitude."*
>
> Jaren L. Davis

I am grateful for: Date   /   /

_____
_____
_____
_____

Things that made me laugh:

_____
_____
_____

Memorable moments:

_____
_____
_____

One word to describe how you're feeling:

_____

A positive thought:

_____
_____
_____

> *"I am happy because I'm grateful. I choose to be grateful. That gratitude allows me to be happy."*
> Will Arnett

I am grateful for: Date   /   /
_____
_____
_____
_____

Things that made me laugh:
_____
_____
_____
_____

Memorable moments:
_____
_____
_____
_____

One word to describe how you're feeling:
_____

A positive thought:
_____
_____
_____

Express your feelings

> *"It is through gratitude for the present moment that the spiritual dimension of life opens up."*
> Eckhart Tolle

I am grateful for: Date   /   /

_____
_____
_____
_____

Things that made me laugh:

_____
_____
_____

Memorable moments:

_____
_____
_____

One word to describe how you're feeling:

_____

A positive thought:

_____
_____
_____

> *"Gratitude is the fairest blossom which springs from the soul."*
>
> Henry Ward Beecher

I am grateful for:		Date / /

_____
_____
_____
_____

Things that made me laugh:

_____
_____
_____

Memorable moments:

_____
_____
_____

One word to describe how you're feeling:

_____

A positive thought:

_____
_____

"Appreciation is a wonderful thing. It makes what is excellent in others belong to us as well."

Voltaire

I am grateful for: Date   /   /

_____
_____
_____

Things that made me laugh:

_____
_____
_____

Memorable moments:

_____
_____
_____

One word to describe how you're feeling:

_____

A positive thought:

_____
_____

> "When eating fruit, remember the one who planted the tree."
>
> Vietnamese Proverb

I am grateful for: Date   /   /

_____
_____
_____
_____

Things that made me laugh:

_____
_____
_____

Memorable moments:

_____
_____
_____

One word to describe how you're feeling:

_____

A positive thought:

_____
_____
_____

> "When we focus on our gratitude, the tide of disappointment goes out and the tide of love rushes in."
>
> Kristin Armstrong

I am grateful for: Date   /   /

_____
_____
_____
_____

Things that made me laugh:

_____
_____
_____

Memorable moments:

_____
_____
_____

One word to describe how you're feeling:

_____

A positive thought:

_____
_____
_____

> *"Silent gratitude isn't much use to anyone."*
> Gladys Bertha

I am grateful for: Date   /   /
_____
_____
_____
_____

Things that made me laugh:
_____
_____
_____

Memorable moments:
_____
_____
_____

One word to describe how you're feeling:
_____

A positive thought:
_____
_____
_____

Go for a walk, observe the environment around you and find something beautiful

> *"Gratitude is happiness double by wonder."*
> G. K. Chesterton

I am grateful for: Date   /   /
_____
_____
_____
_____

Things that made me laugh:
_____
_____
_____

Memorable moments:
_____
_____
_____

One word to describe how you're feeling:
_____

A positive thought:
_____
_____

"The more you express gratitude for what you have, the more likely you will have even more to express gratitude for."
Zig Ziglar

I am grateful for: Date   /   /
_____
_____
_____
_____

Things that made me laugh:
_____
_____
_____

Memorable moments:
_____
_____
_____

One word to describe how you're feeling:
_____

A positive thought:
_____
_____
_____

"Gratitude is a quality similar to electricity: it must be produced and discharged and used up in order to exist at all."

William Faulkner

I am grateful for: Date   /   /

_____
_____
_____
_____

Things that made me laugh:

_____
_____
_____

Memorable moments:

_____
_____
_____

One word to describe how you're feeling:

_____

A positive thought:

_____
_____
_____

Express your feelings

"Gratitude is not only the greatest of virtues, but the parent of all others."

Mascur Tullius Cicero

I am grateful for: Date   /   /

_____
_____
_____
_____

Things that made me laugh:

_____
_____
_____

Memorable moments:

_____
_____
_____

One word to describe how you're feeling:

_____

A positive thought:

_____
_____
_____

"O Lord that lends me life, lend me a heart replete with thankfulness."

William Shakespeare

I am grateful for: Date   /   /

_____
_____
_____
_____

Things that made me laugh:

_____
_____
_____

Memorable moments:

_____
_____
_____

One word to describe how you're feeling:

_____

A positive thought:

_____
_____
_____

> *"Joy is the simplest form of gratitude."*
> Jim Rohn

I am grateful for: Date   /   /

_____
_____
_____
_____

Things that made me laugh:

_____
_____
_____

Memorable moments:

_____
_____
_____

One word to describe how you're feeling:

_____

A positive thought:

_____
_____

> "Gratitude changes the pangs of memory into a tranquil joy."
> Dietrich Bonhoeffer

I am grateful for: Date   /   /

_____
_____
_____
_____

Things that made me laugh:

_____
_____
_____

Memorable moments:

_____
_____
_____

One word to describe how you're feeling:

_____

A positive thought:

_____
_____
_____

"Gratitude makes sense of our past, brings peace for today, and creates a vision for tomorrow."
Melody Beattie

I am grateful for:					Date / /
_____
_____
_____
_____

Things that made me laugh:
_____
_____
_____

Memorable moments:
_____
_____
_____

One word to describe how you're feeling:
_____

A positive thought:
_____
_____
_____

> *"The roots of all goodness lie in the soil of appreciation for goodness."*
> Dalai Lama

I am grateful for: Date   /   /

_____
_____
_____
_____

Things that made me laugh:

_____
_____
_____

Memorable moments:

_____
_____
_____

One word to describe how you're feeling:

_____

A positive thought:

_____
_____

Make a list of your ten best qualities

"Gratitude is a mark of a noble soul and a refined character. We like to be around those who are grateful."

Joseph B. Wirthlin

I am grateful for:	Date / /

_____
_____
_____
_____

Things that made me laugh:

_____
_____
_____

Memorable moments:

_____
_____
_____

One word to describe how you're feeling:

_____

A positive thought:

_____
_____

> *"Two kinds of gratitude: The sudden kind we feel for what we take; the larger kind we feel for what we give."*
> Edwin Arlington Robinson

I am grateful for: Date   /   /

_____
_____
_____
_____

Things that made me laugh:

_____
_____
_____
_____

Memorable moments:

_____
_____
_____
_____

One word to describe how you're feeling:

_____

A positive thought:

_____
_____
_____

"Gratitude is the inward feeling of kindness received."
Henry Van Dyke

I am grateful for: Date   /   /
_____
_____
_____

Things that made me laugh:
_____
_____
_____

Memorable moments:
_____
_____
_____

One word to describe how you're feeling:
_____

A positive thought:
_____
_____
_____

Express your feelings

> *"Gratitude is a duty which ought to be paid, but which none have a right to expect."*
>
> Jean-Jacques Rousseau

I am grateful for: Date   /   /
_____
_____
_____
_____

Things that made me laugh:
_____
_____
_____

Memorable moments:
_____
_____
_____

One word to describe how you're feeling:
_____

A positive thought:
_____
_____
_____

"As we express our gratitude, we must never forget that the highest appreciation is not to utter words, but to live by them."

John F. Kennedy

I am grateful for: Date / /

_____
_____
_____
_____

Things that made me laugh:

_____
_____
_____

Memorable moments:

_____
_____
_____

One word to describe how you're feeling:

_____

A positive thought:

_____
_____
_____

"Gratitude is the sign of noble souls."
Aesop

I am grateful for: Date   /   /
_____
_____
_____
_____

Things that made me laugh:
_____
_____
_____

Memorable moments:
_____
_____
_____

One word to describe how you're feeling:
_____

A positive thought:
_____
_____
_____

30 Days of Gratitude

My most wonderful memory:
_____
_____
_____

Life lesson I will always remember:
_____
_____
_____

3 simple things to be grateful for:
_____
_____
_____

My Thoughts
_____
_____
_____
_____

> *"Thankfulness is the natural impulse to express that feeling. Thanksgiving is the following of that impulse."*
> Henry Van Dyke

I am grateful for: Date   /   /
_____
_____
_____
_____

Things that made me laugh:
_____
_____
_____

Memorable moments:
_____
_____
_____

One word to describe how you're feeling:
_____

A positive thought:
_____
_____
_____

> *"Feeling gratitude and not expressing it is like wrapping a present and not giving it."*
>
> William Arthur Ward

I am grateful for: **Date   /   /**

_____
_____
_____
_____

Things that made me laugh:

_____
_____
_____

Memorable moments:

_____
_____
_____

One word to describe how you're feeling:

_____

A positive thought:

_____
_____
_____

> *"It's a sign of mediocrity when you demonstrate gratitude with moderation."*
> Roberto Benigni

I am grateful for: Date   /   /
_____
_____
_____
_____

Things that made me laugh:
_____
_____
_____

Memorable moments:
_____
_____
_____

One word to describe how you're feeling:
_____

A positive thought:
_____
_____
_____

> *"Gratitude is the most exquisite form of courtesy."*
> Jacques Maritain

I am grateful for: Date   /   /
_____
_____
_____
_____

Things that made me laugh:
_____
_____
_____

Memorable moments:
_____
_____
_____

One word to describe how you're feeling:
_____

A positive thought:
_____
_____

"Gratitude is when memory is stored in the heart and not in the mind."

Lionel Hampton

I am grateful for: Date   /   /

_____
_____
_____
_____

Things that made me laugh:

_____
_____
_____

Memorable moments:

_____
_____
_____

One word to describe how you're feeling:

_____

A positive thought:

_____
_____
_____

> *"Everything we do should be a result of our gratitude for what God has done for us."*
> Lauryn Hill

I am grateful for: Date   / /

_____
_____
_____
_____

Things that made me laugh:

_____
_____
_____

Memorable moments:

_____
_____
_____

One word to describe how you're feeling:

_____

A positive thought:

_____
_____
_____

Dedicate time and energy to help others

> "Happiness is itself a kind of gratitude."
> Joseph Wood Krutch

I am grateful for: Date   /   /

_____
_____
_____
_____

Things that made me laugh:

_____
_____
_____

Memorable moments:

_____
_____
_____

One word to describe how you're feeling:

_____

A positive thought:

_____
_____

"I was complaining that I had no shoes till I met a man who had no feet."
Confucius

I am grateful for: Date   /   /
___
___
___
___

Things that made me laugh:
___
___
___

Memorable moments:
___
___
___

One word to describe how you're feeling:
___

A positive thought:
___
___
___

"Gratitude; my cup overfloweth."
Anonymous

I am grateful for:　　　　　　　　　Date　/　/

_____
_____
_____
_____

Things that made me laugh:

_____
_____
_____

Memorable moments:

_____
_____
_____

One word to describe how you're feeling:

_____

A positive thought:

_____
_____
_____

Express your feelings

> *"Does not the gratitude of the dog put to shame any man who is ungrateful to his benefactors?"*
>
> St. Basil

I am grateful for: Date   /   /

_____

_____

_____

_____

Things that made me laugh:

_____

_____

_____

Memorable moments:

_____

_____

_____

One word to describe how you're feeling:

_____

A positive thought:

_____

_____

_____

> *"Gratitude is riches. Complaint is poverty."*
> Doris Day

I am grateful for: Date   /   /
_____
_____
_____
_____

Things that made me laugh:
_____
_____
_____

Memorable moments:
_____
_____
_____

One word to describe how you're feeling:
_____

A positive thought:
_____
_____
_____

> *"When a person doesn't have gratitude, something is missing in his or her humanity."*
> Elie Wiesel

I am grateful for: **Date** / /

_____
_____
_____
_____

Things that made me laugh:

_____
_____
_____
_____

Memorable moments:

_____
_____
_____
_____

One word to describe how you're feeling:

_____

A positive thought:

_____
_____
_____

"I'm a great believer in luck, and I find the harder I work, the more I have of it."

Thomas Jefferson

I am grateful for: Date   /   /

_____
_____
_____
_____

Things that made me laugh:

_____
_____
_____

Memorable moments:

_____
_____
_____

One word to describe how you're feeling:

_____

A positive thought:

_____
_____
_____

> *"With the new day comes new strength and new thoughts."*
>
> Eleanor Roosevelt

I am grateful for: Date   /   /
_____
_____
_____
_____

Things that made me laugh:
_____
_____
_____
_____

Memorable moments:
_____
_____
_____
_____

One word to describe how you're feeling:
_____

A positive thought:
_____
_____
_____

> *"Things turn out best for people who make the best of the way things turn out."*
> John Wooden

I am grateful for: Date   /   /
_____
_____
_____
_____

Things that made me laugh:
_____
_____
_____

Memorable moments:
_____
_____
_____

One word to describe how you're feeling:
_____

A positive thought:
_____
_____

Stand in front of a mirror and say "I love you"

"It is never too late to be what you might have been."
George Eliot

I am grateful for: Date   /   /
_____
_____
_____

Things that made me laugh:
_____
_____
_____

Memorable moments:
_____
_____
_____

One word to describe how you're feeling:
_____

A positive thought:
_____
_____
_____

"Everyday is a gift, which is why they call it the present."
Alfred Hitchcock

I am grateful for:　　　　　　　　Date　　/　　/
_____
_____
_____
_____

Things that made me laugh:
_____
_____
_____

Memorable moments:
_____
_____
_____

One word to describe how you're feeling:
_____

A positive thought:
_____
_____
_____

> "Strive to be first: First to nod, First to smile, First to compliment, and first to forgive."
>
> Anonymous

I am grateful for: Date   /   /

_____
_____
_____
_____

Things that made me laugh:

_____
_____
_____

Memorable moments:

_____
_____
_____

One word to describe how you're feeling:

_____

A positive thought:

_____
_____
_____

Express your feelings

> "Your success and happiness lie in you."
> Helen Keller

I am grateful for:					Date / /

_____
_____
_____
_____

Things that made me laugh:

_____
_____
_____

Memorable moments:

_____
_____
_____

One word to describe how you're feeling:

_____

A positive thought:

_____
_____
_____

> *"First say to yourself what you would be; and then do what you have to do."*
>
> Epictetus

I am grateful for: Date   /   /

_____
_____
_____
_____

Things that made me laugh:

_____
_____
_____

Memorable moments:

_____
_____
_____

One word to describe how you're feeling:

_____

A positive thought:

_____
_____
_____

"Step through new doors. The majority of the time there's something fantastic on the other side."
Terry Mindock

I am grateful for: Date   /   /
_____
_____
_____
_____

Things that made me laugh:
_____
_____
_____

Memorable moments:
_____
_____
_____

One word to describe how you're feeling:
_____

A positive thought:
_____
_____
_____

"There is always something to be grateful for."
Anonymous

I am grateful for: Date   /   /

_____
_____
_____

Things that made me laugh:

_____
_____
_____

Memorable moments:

_____
_____
_____

One word to describe how you're feeling:

_____

A positive thought:

_____
_____

"Each day, accept everything that comes to you as a gift. At night, mentally give it all back. In this way, you become free."
Daniel Levin

I am grateful for: Date   /   /
_____
_____
_____
_____

Things that made me laugh:
_____
_____
_____

Memorable moments:
_____
_____
_____

One word to describe how you're feeling:
_____

A positive thought:
_____
_____
_____

"When the best things are not possible, the best may be made of those that are."

Richard Hooker

I am grateful for: **Date**   /   /

_____
_____
_____

Things that made me laugh:

_____
_____

Memorable moments:

_____
_____

One word to describe how you're feeling:

_____

A positive thought:

_____
_____

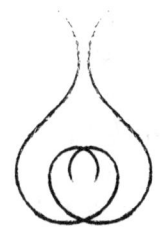

Buy a small present for someone you appreciate

"It doesn't matter how slowly you go so long as you do not stop."

Confucius

I am grateful for:　　　　　　　Date　　/　　/

_____
_____
_____
_____

Things that made me laugh:

_____
_____
_____

Memorable moments:

_____
_____
_____

One word to describe how you're feeling:

_____

A positive thought:

_____
_____
_____

"They can because they think they can."
Virgil

I am grateful for: Date   /   /

_____
_____
_____
_____

Things that made me laugh:

_____
_____
_____

Memorable moments:

_____
_____
_____

One word to describe how you're feeling:

_____

A positive thought:

_____
_____
_____

> *"Almost everything you do will seem insignificant, but it is important that you do it."*
>
> Mahatma Gandhi

I am grateful for: Date   /   /

_____
_____
_____

Things that made me laugh:

_____
_____
_____

Memorable moments:

_____
_____
_____

One word to describe how you're feeling:

_____

A positive thought:

_____
_____

Express your feelings

> *"There is so much to be grateful for,*
> *just open your eyes."*
> Anonymous

I am grateful for: Date   /   /
_____
_____
_____
_____

Things that made me laugh:
_____
_____
_____

Memorable moments:
_____
_____
_____

One word to describe how you're feeling:
_____

A positive thought:
_____
_____
_____

> *"Seek to do good, and you will find that happiness will run after you."*
>
> James Freeman Clarke

I am grateful for:　　　　　　　　Date　　/　　/

_____

_____

_____

Things that made me laugh:

_____

_____

_____

Memorable moments:

_____

_____

_____

One word to describe how you're feeling:

_____

A positive thought:

_____

_____

_____

"Happiness is not a state to arrive at, but a manner of traveling."

Margaret Lee Runbeck

I am grateful for: Date   /   /

_____
_____
_____
_____

Things that made me laugh:

_____
_____
_____

Memorable moments:

_____
_____
_____

One word to describe how you're feeling:

_____

A positive thought:

_____
_____
_____

30 Days of Gratitude

My most wonderful memory:
_____
_____
_____

Funniest moments:
_____
_____
_____

3 beautiful things:
_____
_____
_____

My Thoughts
_____
_____
_____
_____

"Nothing is more honorable than a grateful heart."

Lucius Annaeus Seneca

I am grateful for: Date   /   /
___
___
___
___

Things that made me laugh:
___
___
___

Memorable moments:
___
___
___

One word to describe how you're feeling:
___

A positive thought:
___
___
___

"The only way on earth to multiply happiness is to divide it."

Paul Scherer

I am grateful for: Date   /   /

_____
_____
_____

Things that made me laugh:

_____
_____

Memorable moments:

_____
_____

One word to describe how you're feeling:

_____

A positive thought:

_____
_____

"Why not learn to enjoy the little things. There are so many of them."
Anonymous

I am grateful for: Date   /   /

_____

_____

_____

_____

Things that made me laugh:

_____

_____

_____

Memorable moments:

_____

_____

_____

One word to describe how you're feeling:

_____

A positive thought:

_____

_____

_____

> "Happiness resides not in possessions, and not in gold, happiness dwells in the soul."
> Democritus

I am grateful for:　　　　　　　　Date   /   /

_____
_____
_____
_____

Things that made me laugh:

_____
_____
_____

Memorable moments:

_____
_____
_____

One word to describe how you're feeling:

_____

A positive thought:

_____
_____
_____

> *"For happiness is anyone and anything at all that's loved by you."*
> Charlie Brown

I am grateful for: Date   /   /
_____
_____
_____
_____

Things that made me laugh:
_____
_____
_____

Memorable moments:
_____
_____
_____

One word to describe how you're feeling:
_____

A positive thought:
_____
_____
_____

"Great effort from great motives is the best definition of a happy life."

William Ellery Channing

I am grateful for: Date   /   /

_____

_____

_____

Things that made me laugh:

_____

_____

Memorable moments:

_____

_____

_____

One word to describe how you're feeling:

_____

A positive thought:

_____

_____

_____

Be kind to a stranger

"Life is a shipwreck but we must not forget to sing in the lifeboats."

Voltaire

I am grateful for: Date   /   /

_____
_____
_____

Things that made me laugh:

_____
_____
_____

Memorable moments:

_____
_____
_____

One word to describe how you're feeling:

_____

A positive thought:

_____
_____

"The smallest act of kindness is worth than the grandest invention."

Oscar Wilde

I am grateful for: Date   /   /

_____
_____
_____
_____

Things that made me laugh:

_____
_____
_____

Memorable moments:

_____
_____
_____

One word to describe how you're feeling:

_____

A positive thought:

_____
_____
_____

> "We can change our lives. We can do, have, and be exactly what we wish."
>
> Anthony Robbins

I am grateful for: Date   /   /

_____
_____
_____
_____

Things that made me laugh:

_____
_____
_____

Memorable moments:

_____
_____
_____

One word to describe how you're feeling:

_____

A positive thought:

_____
_____

Express your feelings

"The more I think of it, the more I realize there are no answers. Life is to be lived."

Marilyn Monroe

I am grateful for: Date   /   /
_____
_____
_____
_____

Things that made me laugh:
_____
_____
_____
_____

Memorable moments:
_____
_____
_____
_____

One word to describe how you're feeling:
_____

A positive thought:
_____
_____
_____

> *"It's time to start living the life you've imagined."*
> Henry James

I am grateful for:　　　　　　　　Date　　/　　/

_____
_____
_____

Things that made me laugh:

_____
_____

Memorable moments:

_____
_____

One word to describe how you're feeling:

_____

A positive thought:

_____
_____

> *"Don't let life discourage you; everyone who got where he is had to begin where he was."*
> Richard Evans

I am grateful for:　　　　　　　**Date** __ / __ / __

_____
_____
_____
_____

Things that made me laugh:

_____
_____
_____

Memorable moments:

_____
_____
_____

One word to describe how you're feeling:

_____

A positive thought:

_____
_____
_____

> "The mystery of life is not a problem to be solved but a reality to be experienced."
>
> Art Van Der Leeuw

I am grateful for: Date   /   /
_____
_____
_____

Things that made me laugh:
_____
_____
_____

Memorable moments:
_____
_____
_____

One word to describe how you're feeling:
_____

A positive thought:
_____
_____

"People will forget what you said. People will forget what you did. But people will never forget how you made them feel."
Maya Angelou

I am grateful for: Date   /   /

_____
_____
_____
_____

Things that made me laugh:

_____
_____
_____

Memorable moments:

_____
_____
_____

One word to describe how you're feeling:

_____

A positive thought:

_____
_____
_____

> "Life is 10% what happens to you and 90% how you react to it."
>
> Charles Swindoll

I am grateful for: **Date**   /   /

_____
_____
_____

Things that made me laugh:

_____
_____
_____

Memorable moments:

_____
_____
_____

One word to describe how you're feeling:

_____

A positive thought:

_____
_____

Share positive and encouraging quotes on your social media

> *"Be grateful for what you have and work hard for what you don't have."*
> Anonymous

I am grateful for: Date   /   /
_____
_____
_____
_____

Things that made me laugh:
_____
_____
_____
_____

Memorable moments:
_____
_____
_____
_____

One word to describe how you're feeling:
_____

A positive thought:
_____
_____
_____

"Gratitude is the open door to abundance."
Anonymous

I am grateful for: Date   /   /
_____
_____
_____
_____

Things that made me laugh:
_____
_____
_____

Memorable moments:
_____
_____
_____

One word to describe how you're feeling:
_____

A positive thought:
_____
_____
_____

> *"Take care of your body. It's the only place you have to live."*
>
> Jim Rohn

I am grateful for: Date   /   /

_____
_____
_____
_____

Things that made me laugh:

_____
_____
_____

Memorable moments:

_____
_____
_____

One word to describe how you're feeling:

_____

A positive thought:

_____
_____
_____

Express your feelings

> *"Life is change. Growth is optional. Choose wisely."*
> Anonymous

I am grateful for: Date   /   /
_____
_____
_____
_____

Things that made me laugh:
_____
_____
_____
_____

Memorable moments:
_____
_____
_____
_____

One word to describe how you're feeling:
_____

A positive thought:
_____
_____
_____

"'Enough' is a feast."
Buddhist Proverb

I am grateful for: Date   /   /

_____
_____
_____

Things that made me laugh:

_____
_____
_____

Memorable moments:

_____
_____
_____

One word to describe how you're feeling:

_____

A positive thought:

_____
_____

> *"Start with what is right rather than what is acceptable."*
> Peter F. Drucker

I am grateful for: Date / /
_____
_____
_____
_____

Things that made me laugh:
_____
_____
_____

Memorable moments:
_____
_____
_____

One word to describe how you're feeling:
_____

A positive thought:
_____
_____
_____

"Every great achievement is the victory of a flaming heart."

Ralph Waldo Emerson

I am grateful for: Date   /   /

_____
_____
_____

Things that made me laugh:

_____
_____
_____

Memorable moments:

_____
_____
_____

One word to describe how you're feeling:

_____

A positive thought:

_____
_____
_____

"Don't ever stop dreaming. For people who don't have dreams, don't have much."

Anonymous

I am grateful for: Date   /   /

_____
_____
_____
_____

Things that made me laugh:

_____
_____
_____

Memorable moments:

_____
_____
_____

One word to describe how you're feeling:

_____

A positive thought:

_____
_____
_____

"Don't let today's disappointments cast a shadow on tomorrow's dreams."

James M. Barrie

I am grateful for: Date   /   /

_____
_____
_____
_____

Things that made me laugh:

_____
_____
_____

Memorable moments:

_____
_____
_____

One word to describe how you're feeling:

_____

A positive thought:

_____
_____
_____

● • • • ●

Appreciate all the unique talents and personalities of your colleagues, friends and family

"Success consists of going from failure to failure without loss of enthusiasm."

Winston Churchill

I am grateful for: Date   /   /
_____
_____
_____

Things that made me laugh:
_____
_____
_____

Memorable moments:
_____
_____
_____

One word to describe how you're feeling:
_____

A positive thought:
_____
_____
_____

"Peace begins with a smile."
Mother Teresa

I am grateful for: Date   /   /
_____
_____
_____
_____

Things that made me laugh:
_____
_____
_____

Memorable moments:
_____
_____
_____

One word to describe how you're feeling:
_____

A positive thought:
_____
_____
_____

> *"Kindness, I've discovered, is everything in life."*
> Isaac Bashevis Singer

I am grateful for:　　　　　　　　Date   /   /
_____
_____
_____

Things that made me laugh:
_____
_____
_____

Memorable moments:
_____
_____
_____

One word to describe how you're feeling:
_____

A positive thought:
_____
_____
_____

Express your feelings

"Change your thoughts and you change your world."
Norman Vincent Peale

I am grateful for:　　　　　　　　Date　/　/
_____
_____
_____
_____

Things that made me laugh:
_____
_____
_____
_____

Memorable moments:
_____
_____
_____
_____

One word to describe how you're feeling:
_____

A positive thought:
_____
_____
_____

> "Complaining is silly. Either act or forget."
> Stefan Sagmeister

I am grateful for: Date   /   /
_____
_____
_____

Things that made me laugh:
_____
_____
_____

Memorable moments:
_____
_____
_____

One word to describe how you're feeling:
_____

A positive thought:
_____
_____

> *"No one can make you feel inferior without your consent."*
> Rosa Parks

I am grateful for:　　　　　　　　Date　　/　　/

_____
_____
_____
_____

Things that made me laugh:

_____
_____
_____

Memorable moments:

_____
_____
_____

One word to describe how you're feeling:

_____

A positive thought:

_____
_____
_____

30 Days of Gratitude

My most wonderful memory:
_____
_____
_____

Special moments with friends or family:
_____
_____
_____

3 hobbies that make you happy:
_____
_____
_____

My Thoughts
_____
_____
_____
_____

Remember, be thankful always for all that you have!

Please, remember to write a sincere review.

www.ingramcontent.com/pod-product-compliance
Lightning Source LLC
Chambersburg PA
CBHW072203100526
44589CB00015B/2341